West Chicago Public Library District
118 West Washington
West Chicago, IL 60185-2803
Phone # (630) 231-1552

VELOCIRAPTOR

By Susan H. Gray

THE CHILD'S WORLD®
CHANHASSEN, MINNESOTA

Published in the United States of America by The Child's World®
P.O. Box 326, Chanhassen, MN 55317-0326
800-599-READ
www.childsworld.com

Content Adviser:
Peter Makovicky,
Ph.D., Curator,
Field Museum,
Chicago, Illinois

Photo Credits: #217575, Rota/American Museum of Natural History Library: 16; David Muench/Corbis: 13; Vo Trung Dung/Corbis Sygma: 14; Hulton-Deutsch Collection/Corbis: 18, 20; Tom Bean/Corbis: 22; Corbis Sygma: 23; James L. Amos/Corbis: 26; Culver Pictures, Inc.: 25; AFP Photo/D. Finnen, American Museum of Natural History/Getty Images: 6; Laski Diffusion/EastNews/Liaison/Getty Images: 11; Joe Tucciarone/Science Photo Library/Photo Researchers, Inc.: 5, 19; Francois Gohier/Photo Researchers, Inc.: 10 (Specimen Courtesy Gaston Design), 21, 24 (Specimen from College of Eastern Utah Prehistoric Museum, Price UT); Biophoto Associates/Photo Researchers, Inc.: 15; Ken Lucas/Visuals Unlimited, Inc.: 7, 9.

The Child's World®: Mary Berendes, Publishing Director

Editorial Directions, Inc.: E. Russell Primm, Editorial Director; Dana Meachen Rau, Line Editor; Katie Marsico, Assistant Editor; Matthew Messbarger, Editorial Assistant; Susan Hindman, Copy Editor; Susan Ashley, Proofreader; Tim Griffin, Indexer; Kerry Reid, Fact Checker; Dawn Friedman, Photo Reseacher; Linda S. Koutris, Photo Selector

Original cover art by Todd Marshall

The Design Lab: Kathleen Petelinsek, Design and Page Production

Library of Congress Cataloging-in-Publication Data
Gray, Susan Heinrichs.
  Velociraptor / by Susan H. Gray.
    p. cm. — (Exploring dinosaurs)
Includes index.
Contents: Dying for something to eat—What is a Velociraptor?—What are fossils?—How did Velociraptor get its name?—What kinds of fossils did Velociraptor leave behind?—The Cretaceous Period.
  ISBN 1-59296-047-2 (lib. bdg. : alk. paper)
 1. Velociraptor—Juvenile literature. [1. Velociraptor. 2. Dinosaurs.] I. Title. II. Series.
QE862.S3G696 2004
567.912—dc22   2003018634

TABLE OF CONTENTS

CHAPTER ONE

DYING FOR SOMETHING TO EAT

The afternoon sun beat down. Warm breezes whipped up a

sandstorm. The *Velociraptor* (vuh-LAHS-ih-RAP-ter) squint-

ed its eyes in the wind. This alert little dinosaur heard a noise and

quickly turned his head toward the sound. There, in the distance,

stood dinner—a *Protoceratops* (PRO-toe-SER-uh-tops).

The *Protoceratops* buried his head in some bushy plants and

munched away. The *Velociraptor* tensed his muscles. He leaned for-

ward, then raced toward his **prey.** The *Protoceratops* raised his

head, but it was too late. The *Velociraptor* was already upon it.

The *Velociraptor's* powerful feet kicked at the heavy animal's

belly. His fierce claw tore into the throat. Then the *Protoceratops*

clamped the attacker's arm in his mouth. The two locked in combat.

*In addition to its speed, deadly claws, and sharp teeth, Velociraptor is believed
to have been among the most intelligent of the dinosaurs.*

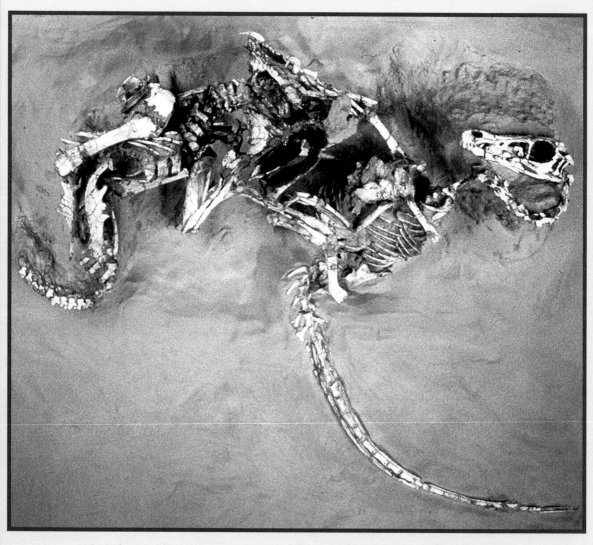

These dinosaur remains show a Velociraptor *and a* Protoceratops *locked in battle.* Protoceratops *was no match for* Velociraptor's *hunting skills.*

As they struggled, the wind grew stronger. Sand swept in and buried

the animals up to their knees. Still they wrestled. The hot sand rose

higher and higher. At last they were completely covered.

CHAPTER TWO

WHAT IS A
VELOCIRAPTOR?

ighty million years after the two dinosaurs were buried, scientists found their skeletons still locked in battle. Skeletons tell us a lot about a dinosaur's life. *Velociraptor* bones show that it was a small dinosaur. It was probably no more than 6 feet (1.8 meters)

A model of two Velociraptors *on the chase. Scientists know* Velociraptor *could run quickly for short distances, but they also believe it may have been able to jump.*

long from the snout to the tip of the tail. Scientists think it weighed

35 to 60 pounds (16 to 27 kilograms). When it stood, it was proba-

bly only 3 to 4 feet (0.9 to 1.2 m) tall.

The little **reptile** had strong, muscular legs built for running.

As it ran, it held its tail stiff and straight out in back for balance.

Velociraptor, like a bird, had a unique wrist joint that may have allowed

it to hold its long arms folded up, much like wings. Some scientists

think that for short bursts, *Velociraptor* could run about 25 miles

(40 kilometers) per hour.

Velociraptor's feet carried its deadliest weapons—the claws. Every

finger and toe had a claw, but the second toe of each foot was espe-

cially well armed. It had a fierce curved claw that was up to 4 inches

(10 centimeters) long. As the dinosaur trotted along, it held these

two big claws off the ground. But when *Velociraptor* tensed its toe

Why did Velociraptor *trot without letting its two large claws touch the ground? Scientists think this behavior helped keep the dangerous nails extra sharp.*

muscles, the claws swung down with frightening force. These

weapons were perfect for snagging prey and tearing it apart.

Velociraptor had an unusually large head for its small body.

This Velociraptor *skull shows how sharp the dinosaur's teeth were.*
Some Velociraptor *teeth were more than 1 inch (2.5 cm) long.*

Its jaws were muscular and filled with sharp teeth. The presence

of many sharp teeth tells us that this dinosaur ate meat.

The animal's skull had two big eye sockets. Therefore,

Velociraptor probably had large eyes and good vision. The big space

in the skull shows us that the dinosaur had a large brain. The animal

lived from about 85 million to 80 million years ago.

CHAPTER THREE

WHAT ARE FOSSILS?

The fossils of the battling dinosaurs are among the most

amazing discoveries of paleontology (PAY-lee-un-TAWL-

uh-jee). Fossils are the remains of **ancient** plants and animals.

Dinosaur eggs, ancient clamshells, and *Velociraptor* bones are

These dinosaur eggs are fossils. Eggs that contain baby dinosaurs that never hatched are some of the rarest fossils ever discovered.

examples of fossils. Paleontology is the study of fossils and ancient life.

The word *fossil* comes from a Latin word that means "dug up." Not all fossils are dug up, however. Many fossils are only partly buried in rocks. Some are found lying out in the open. Wind and rain have uncovered them.

Very, very few dinosaur bones have been **preserved** as fossils. This is because several things must take place before any part of a dinosaur can be preserved. First, the animal must be buried. Dinosaurs might sink into soft mud. They might be covered in sand, like the struggling *Velociraptor.* Once buried, they cannot be torn apart by other animals. Wind and rain cannot wear them away. Over time, their soft tissues rot away. Their hard parts, such as bones, teeth, and claws, remain.

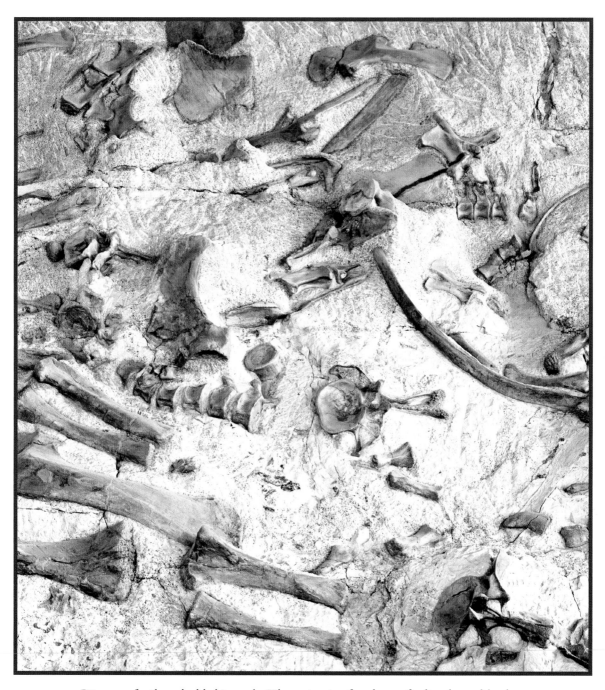

*Dinosaur fossils embedded in rock. When scientists first began finding bones like these,
they used pickaxes to dig them out and then loaded them onto horse-drawn carts.
Because of this rough handling, many bones were damaged or broken.*

Over time, these Velociraptor *bones became fossilized. You can see here some of the deadly claws the dinosaur would have used to hunt with while it was alive.*

Next, the animal's hard parts must become **fossilized.** There

are several ways this can happen. One way is by hard **minerals** in

the environment seeping into small holes in the bones. This makes

them very hard. Another way is when mineral **molecules** replace the bone molecules, one by one.

A third way an animal's hard parts become fossilized is by natural molds and casts. First, a bone becomes buried, then it **dissolves**

A mold and cast of Ellipsocephalus. *This prehistoric creature was a hard-shelled animal that lived in the water.*

away. It leaves a **cavity** behind, surrounded by rocky material.

The rocky material becomes the mold of the bone. It shows exactly where the bone was. If the cavity fills in with new material that hardens, this is a cast. The cast will look just like the bone that dissolved away.

MAKING DINOSAUR COPIES

Scientists often make their own molds and casts of dinosaur bones. To do this, they first carefully clean the real bone. Then they pour a soft material, such as liquid rubber, on one side of the bone. Soon the material dries, and the scientists take out the bone, leaving behind the shape of the bone in the rubber. This is called the mold. Scientists then repeat the process for the other side of the bone.

When the two parts of the mold are put together, there is a bone-shaped space inside. The scientists pour another material into this space. This might be liquid plastic or something else that hardens as it dries. As soon as it is dry, the scientists peel the rubber mold away. Inside lies a perfect cast, or copy, of the bone.

Paleontologists make copies of dinosaur bones for several reasons. They give copies to other scientists around the world, so they can study the dinosaur. They give copies to museums so they can build dinosaur exhibits. And they study the copies themselves, when the real bones are too delicate.

CHAPTER FOUR

How Did *Velociraptor* Get Its Name?

It takes a long time for a dinosaur—or any animal—to get a name. When scientists discover a new dinosaur, they study it very closely. They look at its body parts. They look at where it was found. They try to figure out when it lived. They think about what it ate and how it spent its time. And they compare it to other dinosaurs they already know about.

Once they have decided that the dinosaur is different from all other known dinosaurs, scientists pick out its name. They choose a first and last name. Often, these names tell something about the animal. Sometimes they tell where the dinosaur was found. Sometimes a dinosaur is named after the person who found it. *Velociraptor* is the dinosaur's first name. Its last name is

A camel train in Mongolia during the 1920s, around the same time the first Velociraptor *skeleton was discovered there.* Velociraptor *also lived in what are now Russia and China.*

mongoliensis (mon-GOLE-ee-EN-sis). This means it lived in

Mongolia.

After an animal's name is chosen, there is still more work to do.

Scientists from around the world have to agree that this name is

okay. They check to see if any other animal has the same name. For

Velociraptor, it was agreed that the name was fine. So *Velociraptor*

mongoliensis became official.

Scientists also need to decide which larger group of dinosaurs a new dinosaur belongs to. This gives them a picture of how all the dinosaurs in that group are related. To make this decision, they compare how the new dinosaur is like some dinosaurs they know of and how it is different.

Paleontologists decided that *Velociraptor* fit into a group known as the deinonychosaurs (DINE-oh-NIKE-uh-sawrz). These dinosaurs ran about on two legs and ate meat. They also had big, deadly claws on their feet. The deinony-chosaurs came in many different sizes. Scientists knew that *Velociraptor* fit into this group.

These two dinosaurs are deinonychosaurs. Another trait shared by all deinonychosaurs was that they could run at higher speeds for short distances, but were unable to chase prey for longer stretches.

CHAPTER FIVE

WHAT KINDS OF FOSSILS DID *VELOCIRAPTOR* LEAVE BEHIND?

Velociraptor skeletons have been found in Mongolia, Russia, and China. Only a few skeletons of the creature have been found. The first one was found in Mongolia. Paleontologist Henry Osborn wrote about it in 1924. He named it *Velociraptor,* which means "quick thief," because he believed it stole other dinosaurs' eggs.

In 1971, a team of paleontologists found the battling *Velociraptor* and *Protoceratops*

Paleontologist Roy Chapman Andrews examines dinosaur eggs he found in Mongolia during the 1920s. Andrews uncovered the first Velociraptor *skeleton. Because of his work, Andrews has been referred to as the "Dragon Hunter."*

These famous skeletons show Velociraptor *and* Protoceratops *battling one another. Before they were buried in sand,* Velociraptor *succeeded in using its sharp claws to tear out the throat and belly of its prey.*

skeletons. This find was in the Gobi Desert in Mongolia. Such a dry,

sandy area was perfect for fossilization to take place.

Velociraptor also left footprints behind. By studying footprints,

experts can often tell how fast a dinosaur moved. They can also tell

whether it traveled in a group. Scientists have decided that while

Fossils of skeletons tell scientists about a dinosaur's body, but fossils of footprints help determine the activities and habits of the animal while it was alive.

Velociraptor was fast, it was probably slower than some other

meat-eating dinosaurs related to it. They are not sure yet whether

Velociraptor traveled alone or in a group.

DON'T BELIEVE EVERYTHING YOU SEE!

In the 1990s, theaters showed a movie called *Jurassic Park.*
In the movie, *Velociraptors* ran over hills and through
forests. They were very smart, cunning animals. They
hunted in packs. Each one was taller than an adult human.
People who saw the movie did not see what *Velociraptor*
was really like. Dinosaur experts knew that the movie

showed an animal that never existed.

However, while the movie was being made, a new dinosaur was discovered in Utah. It looked a lot like *Velociraptor,* but it was taller than a grown man. Paleontologists gave it the name *Utahraptor* (YOO-tah-RAP-ter). They decided it was related to *Velociraptor.* It may have looked a lot like the dinosaur in the movie. So maybe the *Jurassic Park* animal existed after all. It just had the wrong name.

There is still one big problem, though—the name of the movie. The Jurassic period of time was from 208 million to 144 million years ago. Neither *Utahraptor* nor *Velociraptor* existed during this time. They did not appear until millions of years later!

CHAPTER SIX

THE CRETACEOUS PERIOD

The Earth has been around for millions of years. Scientists who study the Earth have divided up all those years into groups. For example, one group of years is called the Triassic (try-ASS-ik) period. This was from about 248 million to 208 million years ago.

A drawing of Ceratosaurus, *a dinosaur that lived during the late Jurassic period.* Ceratosaurus *was a cunning meat eater capable of killing much larger animals.*

This fossil of a dragonfly is from the late Cretaceous period. Dragonflies actually appeared earlier than the Cretaceous period, but fossils show that they grew smaller over time. At first, their wingspans were up to 27.5 inches (70 cm) long!

Dinosaurs first appeared during this time. The Jurassic period came next. It was from about 208 million to 144 million years ago. Then came the Cretaceous (kreh-TAY-shuss) period. It was from about 144 million to 65 million years ago. *Velociraptor* lived during this period. At the time, dinosaurs ruled the Earth. But other animals were starting to appear. The first ants crawled about, and the first butterflies flitted from plant to plant. Little mammals that looked a lot like opossums nosed about the ground. Flying and diving birds appeared. Flowering plants began to spring up. Forests of oaks and maples began to spread.

At the end of the Cretaceous period, 65 million years ago, dinosaurs and many other animals suddenly died out. No one is certain why this happened. Perhaps it was because more and more volcanoes were becoming active. Maybe they filled the air with too much dust and ash. Perhaps the Earth was becoming too hot or too cold for dinosaurs to live. Perhaps a giant asteroid hit the Earth. Although no one knows the answer, everyone agrees on one thing. The "age of the dinosaurs" had come to an end.

Scientists are working hard to figure out why the dinosaurs vanished. They are also trying to learn more about the life of little *Velociraptor.* Did it hunt in packs? Did it steal other dinosaurs' eggs? Just how fast could it run? Paleontologists would love to know the answers to these questions. Perhaps one day you will become the scientist who solves these mysteries.

Glossary

ancient (AYN-shunt) Something that is ancient is very old; from millions of years ago. Fossils are the remains of ancient plants and animals.

cavity (KAV-uh-tee) A cavity is a hole. When an animal bone becomes buried, it often breaks down and leaves a cavity behind.

dissolves (di-ZOLVZ) When something dissolves, it breaks down and slowly disappears. A buried animal bone might dissolve, leaving a cavity behind.

exhibits (eg-ZIB-itz) Exhibits are objects that are shown in public. Exhibits of dinosaur bones can often be seen in museums.

fossilized (FOSS-uhl-ized) When something is fossilized, it becomes a fossil. An animal's bones can be fossilized by natural molds and casts.

minerals (MIN-ur-uhlz) Minerals are hard materials found in the ground. Minerals contribute to a dead animal's parts becoming fossilized.

molecules (MOL-uh-kyoolz) Molecules are the smallest parts of a substance that display all the chemical traits of that substance. Mineral molecules replace bone molecules as part of the fossilization process.

preserved (pri-ZURVD) Something that is preserved is saved. Very few dinosaurs that walked the Earth have been preserved as fossils.

prey (PRAY) Prey are animals that are eaten by other animals. *Velociraptor*'s claws were perfect for snagging prey and tearing it apart.

reptile (REP-tile) A reptile is an air-breathing animal with a backbone and is usually covered with scales or plates. *Velociraptor* was a reptile.

Did You Know?

▸ The fighting skeletons of *Protoceratops* and *Velociraptor* have been named a national treasure of Mongolia.

▸ *Velociraptor* belongs to a group of dinosaurs called the raptors. All of them had the large killing claws on their feet.

The Geologic Time Scale

TRIASSIC PERIOD

Date: 248 million to 208 million years ago

Fossils: *Coelophysis, Cynodont, Desmatosuchus, Eoraptor, Gerrothorax, Peteinosaurus, Placerias, Plateosaurus, Postosuchus, Procompsognathus, Riojasaurus, Saltopus, Teratosaurus, Thecodontosaurus*

Distinguishing Features: For the most part, the climate in the Triassic period was hot and dry. The first true mammals appeared during this period, as well as turtles, frogs, salamanders, and lizards. Corals could also be found in oceans at this time, although large reefs such as the ones we have today did not yet exist. Evergreen trees made up much of the plant life.

JURASSIC PERIOD

Date: 208 million to 144 million years ago

Fossils: *Allosaurus, Anchisaurus, Apatosaurus, Barosaurus, Brachiosaurus, Ceratosaurus, Compsognathus, Cryptoclidus, Dilophosaurus, Diplodocus, Eustreptospondylus, Hybodus, Janenschia, Kentrosaurus, Liopleurodon, Megalosaurus, Opthalmosaurus, Rhamphorhynchus, Saurolophus, Segisaurus, Seismosaurus, Stegosaurus, Supersaurus, Syntarsus, Ultrasaurus, Vulcanodon, Xiaosaurus*

Distinguishing Features: The climate of the Jurassic period was warm and moist. The first birds appeared during this period. Plant life was also greener and more widespread. Sharks began swimming in Earth's oceans. Although dinosaurs didn't even exist at the beginning of the Triassic period, they ruled Earth by Jurassic times. There was a minor mass extinction toward the end of the Jurassic period.

CRETACEOUS PERIOD

Date: 144 million to 65 million years ago

Fossils: *Acrocanthosaurus, Alamosaurus, Albertosaurus, Anatotitan, Ankylosaurus, Argentinosaurus, Bagaceratops, Baryonyx, Carcharodontosaurus, Carnotaurus, Centrosaurus, Chasmosaurus, Corythosaurus, Didelphodon, Edmontonia, Edmontosaurus, Gallimimus, Gigantosaurus, Hadrosaurus, Hypsilophodon, Iguanodon, Kronosaurus, Lambeosaurus, Leaellynasaura, Maiasaura, Megaraptor, Muttaburrasaurus, Nodosaurus, Ornithocheirus, Oviraptor, Pachycephalosaurus, Panoplosaurus, Parasaurolophus, Pentaceratops, Polacanthus, Protoceratops, Psittacosaurus, Quaesitosaurus, Saltasaurus, Sarcosuchus, Saurolophus, Sauropelta, Saurornithoides, Segnosaurus, Spinosaurus, Stegoceras, Stygimoloch, Styracosaurus, Tapejara, Tarbosaurus, Therizinosaurus, Thescelosaurus, Torosaurus, Trachodon, Triceratops, Troodon, Tyrannosaurus rex, Utahraptor, Velociraptor*

Distinguishing Features: The climate of the Cretaceous period was fairly mild. Flowering plants first appeared in this period, and many modern plants developed. With flowering plants came a greater diversity of insect life. Birds further developed into two types: flying and flightless. A wider variety of mammals also existed. At the end of this period came a great mass extinction that wiped out the dinosaurs, along with several other groups of animals.

How to Learn More

At the Library

Dingus, Lowell, and Mark A. Norell. *Searching for Velociraptor.*
New York: HarperCollins Children's Books, 1996.

Landau, Elaine. *Velociraptor.* Danbury, Conn.: Children's Press, 1999.

Lessem, Don, and David Peters (illustrator). *Raptors!: The Nastiest Dinosaurs.*
Boston: Little Brown & Co. 1998.

On the Web

Visit our home page for lots of links about *Velociraptor:*
http://www.childsworld.com/links.html
Note to Parents, Teachers, and Librarians: We routinely verify our
Web links to make sure they're safe, active sites—so encourage
your readers to check them out!

Places to Visit or Contact

AMERICAN MUSEUM OF NATURAL HISTORY
To view numerous dinosaur fossils, as well as
the fossils of several ancient mammals
Central Park West at 79th Street
New York, NY 10024-5192
212/769-5100

CARNEGIE MUSEUM OF NATURAL HISTORY
To view a variety of dinosaur skeletons, as well as fossils related
to other reptiles, amphibians, and fish that are now extinct
4400 Forbes Avenue
Pittsburgh, PA 15213
412/622-3131

DINOSAUR NATIONAL MONUMENT

To view a huge deposit of dinosaur bones in a natural setting

4545 East Highway 40

Dinosaur, CO 81610-9724

or

DINOSAUR NATIONAL MONUMENT (QUARRY)

11625 East 1500 South

Jensen, UT 84035

435/781-7700

MUSEUM OF THE ROCKIES

To see real dinosaur fossils, as well as robotic replicas

Montana State University

600 West Kagy Boulevard

Bozeman, MT 59717-2730

406/994-2251 or 406/994-DINO (3466)

NATIONAL MUSEUM OF NATURAL HISTORY

(SMITHSONIAN INSTITUTION)

To see several dinosaur exhibits and special behind-the-scenes tours

10th Street and Constitution Avenue, N.W.

Washington, DC 20560-0166

202/357-2700

Index

About the Author

Susan H. Gray has bachelor's and master's degrees in zoology, and has taught college-level courses in biology. She first fell in love with fossil hunting while studying paleontology in college. In her 25 years as an author, she has written many articles for scientists and researchers, and many science books for children. Susan enjoys gardening, traveling, and playing the piano. She and her husband, Michael, live in Cabot, Arkansas.